All About

Conte

Introduction

The ferret is a very misunderstood animal. It was once reputed to be both vicious and evil-smelling but, in fact, the ferret it is a delightful, intelligent, fun-loving, affectionate creature.

Ferrets have been domesticated for approximately 2,500 years. They are carnivores and members of the *Mustelid* family, which includes weasels, polecats, stoats, mink, martens, badgers and otters.

Where Do Ferrets Come From?

The ferret (*Mustela putorius furo*) is thought to be a domestication of the European Polecat (*Mustela putorius*). The rabbit was a native species in a number of Mediterranean countries, and this is probably where the ferret also originated. It was introduced to Britain by the Romans, more than likely to exterminate rodents.

By the Middle Ages, the ferret was well-established as a domestic animal, and was later transported to North America by European colonists.

The Ferret As A Pet

POSITIVES
• The natural temperament is one of friendliness and curiosity.
• Ferrets make entertaining companions. They enjoy human

company, and they can be harness-trained.

• Ferrets are clean animals, and can be house-trained.

Ferrets are friendly and sociable animals.

NEGATIVES

• Ferrets can be destructive. They will uproot pot plants, dig holes in carpets and soft furnishings, or rearrange ornaments and bookshelves.
• A ferret that has been mistreated or mishandled can give a nasty bite.
• Odour. All animals have their own characteristic smell and the ferret is no exception. However the strong, musky smell of the entire male can be greatly reduced by neutering.

Ferrets And Children

Very young children and ferrets are not a good combination. Young children do not always recognise the warning signals when an animal has had enough and could push the ferret too far. This could result in the ferret nipping a child.

The best time to introduce a ferret to the family is when a child is around ten years old, and understands how to treat an animal correctly. Even then, adult supervision is recommended as much for the sake of the ferret as the child.

Older children will appreciate how to care for and handle a ferret.

Understanding Ferrets

Ferrets may be descended from wild polecats, but domestication has dramatically changed their behaviour. The polecat is a solitary animal whereas most ferrets tend to prefer the company of humans and their own kind. Polecats are shy, whereas ferrets are curious and approach most situations with little fear.

Although ferrets are comparatively poor at killing wild prey, do not forget that the ferret is still a predator, with the instincts of a predator. Given the opportunity, it will attack, and may even kill, small mammals and birds.

Characteristics

Ferrets can be extremely singled-minded in their approach to life. Trying to persuade your ferret not to scratch at the carpet or not to knock ornaments off a shelf can be an uphill struggle. You may not win the argument! Here are five aspects of ferret behaviour to look for:

• Always expect the unexpected with a ferret. It has been said that ferrets don't climb or jump but, in fact, most will do both.

• A ferret is inquisitive and normally fearless, and could soon find trouble if he should escape from home.

• When a ferret is really excited,

he appears to 'dance'. He will move sideways, jumping and twisting, with his mouth open making a staccato chuckling noise (known as 'chooking'), which means he is happy. Some even make a 'hee-hee' panting sound, which is another happy, contented ferret noise.

• A high-pitched chattering can indicate pain. This could happen during rough play with another ferret, when it could also mean "you are standing on my paw!"

• A soft hissing (similar to a cat's hiss of anger) is a warning that the ferret is not happy with the situation and wishes to be left alone.

Ferret Odour

All ferrets have a number of small scent glands all over their body. However, these do not produce offensive or powerful odours; the ferret is characterised by a musky smell, which becomes less noticeable in neutered ferrets.

Ferrets do have larger, scent-producing anal glands, and these can release a very unpleasant smell if the ferret is frightened or is attacked. De-scenting surgery is an option, but is not recommended by me or by the British Small Animal Veterinary Association. It is only very occasionally that a ferret is frightened enough to 'spray', and most ferret owners agree that de-scenting in unnecessary. It may even seriously affect the animals general health and well-being.

Life Expectancy

A well-kept ferret can be expected to live from six to ten years; a few may reach twelve, or beyond.

Choosing A Ferret

Before deciding to buy a ferret, remember that you are taking on a big responsibility.

• Your ferret will need to be cared for on a daily basis throughout his life. This means making special arrangements for even the briefest holiday.

• You must find a vet who is prepared to accept a ferret as a patient, and who has the specialised knowledge to treat him.

Life with a ferret is fun, but it is also a tie, and you must be prepared to accept this before taking the plunge into ownership.

Where To Go

Find out as much as you can about ferret clubs in your area. Your local library should have information. A club will put you in touch with ferret breeders, and this is a good source for obtaining your first youngster (kit). The advantage is that you will be able to see the parents, and will probably get a lot of advice from the breeder when making your choice.

If you have a ferret rescue shelter in your area, they may well have kits or suitable adults available. You can also buy direct from a pet shop. Make sure the store you visit is well-run, and the staff are knowledgeable.

What Age?

Ideally, the kits should be twelve weeks old before leaving their mother. Ferret kits are weaned at six to ten weeks old, but the extra few weeks they are left with their mother can make a world of difference to them, especially in terms of building confidence.

Pet, Show or Working?

Pet ferrets, show ferrets and working ferrets should be one and the same animal. A well-kept ferret should be capable of performing all three functions, although the majority of ferret owners may not be interested in the working side.

Male or Female?

The hob (male) ferret is usually larger than the jill (female). The obvious difference is the sexual organs. The penis is some distance away from the anus of the hob; the vulva and anus of the jill are close together.

Entire hobs (i.e. un-neutered) have a stronger odour than jills, especially in the breeding season. In the case of hobs, this starts in December and runs through until June. During this time the hob will become aggressive towards other entire males and will start dragging females around by their necks. The hob should be kept alone during this period.

Male.

Female.

These problems can be solved if the hob is castrated. This should be carried out once the ferret is over six months old.

Entire jills will stay in oestrus from Spring until autumn, unless they are brought out by mating, the use of a vasectomised hob, or by a hormone injection. Jills left in season run the risk of an infection or developing aplastic anaemia, which is usually fatal. If a jill is not going to be use for breeding, she should be spayed when she is six months old.

Signs of a healthy ferret

It is imperative that the kit you buy is fit and healthy. Look for the following signs:

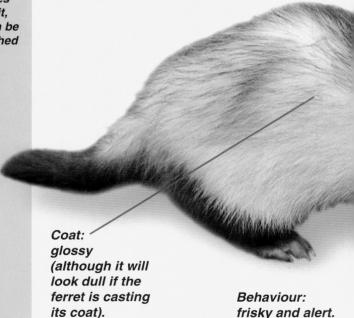

Coat: glossy (although it will look dull if the ferret is casting its coat).

Behaviour: frisky and alert.

More Than One?

Most ferrets enjoy the company of their own kind. In fact, the only thing better than one ferret is two ferrets. It does not matter which sexes you keep, providing they have been neutered or spayed.

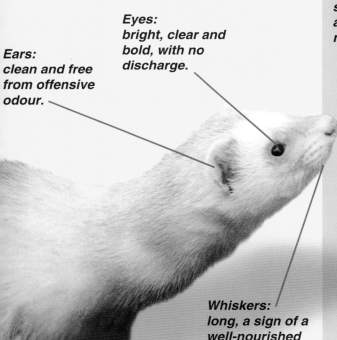

Nose:
slightly damp and cool, with no discharge.

Eyes:
bright, clear and bold, with no discharge.

Ears:
clean and free from offensive odour.

Whiskers:
long, a sign of a well-nourished ferret.

Colours And Markings

Health and temperament should always come before colour when selecting a ferret. However, you may have a preference, particularly if you are planning a breeding programme.

Ferrets can change their colour and markings throughout their life. A ferret could be a polecat Silver-mitt and, a couple of years later, he is more like a Silver. Some ferrets change their markings with the season.

The classification of colours may vary from country to country.

Albino

The Albino is often regarded as the 'true ferret'. The coat is pale, ranging from pure-white to cream, and these ferrets always have red eyes. They are also known as Red-eyed Whites. Not as common are Black or Dark-eyed Whites, which are pale-coated with black, dark blue or brown eyes.

Sable/Polecat

The sable or polecat ferret is so called because it has the markings of a wild polecat, not because it is bred from true polecats. They have a dark mask across the eyes and dark coloured limbs and tail. The colour of the body may also be very dark, but they may have dark guard hairs over a light undercoat. This is a very popular colour.

Silver-mitt

These ferrets are so called because of their white feet, even though they can also have polecat markings. Some have white or cream bibs or throat flashes, and some may have pale face markings or a blaze like a badger.

DID YOU KNOW?

It is untrue that using a ferret for hunting or feeding it raw meat, makes it vicious.

Silver/Sterling Silver

These are pale-coated with darker tips to each hair, giving a frosted, silver appearance. These ferrets frequently have very dark eyes. They are strikingly attractive, and although once quite rare, they are now more readily available. The can range from a very light silver to the colour of gun metal.

DID YOU KNOW?

If you hold a ferret by the scruff of the neck it will yawn.

Sandy/Butterscotch/Cinnamon

The colour ranges from pale gold to deep red. Some have a polecat mask.
Eyes dark to red.

Hutch

This should be as large as possible. A good-sized rabbit hutch (4ft x 2ft x 2ft), with modifications, such as reducing the entrance to the sleeping quarters to a ferret-sized hole, will provide accommodation for two ferrets. The hutch should be waterproof and draught-proof; ferrets can stand cold better than draughts and damp.

The hutch must be fitted with a welded-mesh front.

Make sure it is strong enough to keep the ferret in! The front of the cage should be welded mesh, as a ferret will make short work of chicken wire, and can wriggle out of a one-inch gap.

The hutch should be placed in sheltered area. Protect the cage from fierce sunshine in the summer as ferrets do not sweat, and the build-up of heat within the cage will cause heatstroke which, if left untreated, will prove fatal.

Cage

Indoor cages suitable for ferrets can be obtained from a pet store. Buy the largest one you can afford – ferrets need plenty of room. It is possible to buy two or three-floor type 'condos', where the floors are connected with ramps.

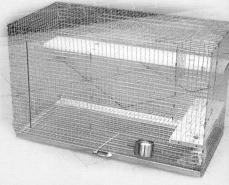

Buy the largest cage you can afford.

If the cage has wire floors and ramps, they must be covered with carpet, plywood or something similar. Walking on wire will harm your ferret's feet, and it could end up ripping out a nail or breaking a toe if its foot gets trapped between the wires.

Outside Run

Again, an outside run should be as large as possible. Welded mesh should be used in the construction, not chicken wire. If the run is to be placed on hard-standing, such as concrete or flags, it will not need a base. If it is to be placed on grass or soil it will require either a mesh or wooden base.

If the run is to be a permanent fixture, remove one foot of soil and bury welded mesh, extending the sides of the run. This will allow your ferrets to dig holes, yet still be safe and secure inside the run.

The ferret is a great escape artist, so his home must be both comfortable and secure.

Types Of Bedding

Straw and hay can be used, but may carry mites or ticks, while shredded paper (not newspaper) is fine. Old T-shirts and towels make excellent bedding. It should be changed or washed weekly.

DID YOU KNOW?

The ribs of a ferret are so supple that it can crawl through spaces that look far too narrow by flattening itself.

Equipment

Hammock

Ferrets love relaxing and sleeping in a hammock. You can buy them ready to clip on to the bars of the cage.

Litter Pan

This should be located on the ground floor. Wood pellets are excellent, but most cat litters, except the clumping type, will do. You can even line the tray with old newspapers, but these will need changing more frequently.

Feeding Utensils

A heavy ceramic bowl is needed, as the first thing a ferret does with a light food bowl is turn it upside-down. For water, a gravity-fed bottle is preferable.

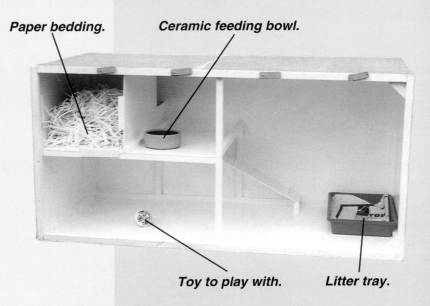

Paper bedding.

Ceramic feeding bowl.

Toy to play with.

Litter tray.

Toys

Toys that have been specially designed for ferrets are now stocked in pet stores, and they can provide a lot of fun and entertainment. However, ferrets can be kept amused by the simplest things: a cardboard box with holes cut in it can provide lots of fun, a supermarket carrier bag is a great favourite (the ferret loves the noise it makes), carpet tubes and drain pipes are loved by all ferrets.

There are a variety of toys that have been specially designed for ferrets.

Harness And Lead

The best type of harness to buy is the "H" type where one smaller strap is fastened round the neck of the ferret and the other around the chest. It must be a snug fit which does not give the ferret any chance of wriggling free.

Carrier

You will need a small pet carrier. The type used for cats will be ideal for transporting your ferret home. Old T-shirts or towels can be used as lining. Ferrets love snuggling into warm soft bedding and this will reduce any stress of travelling.

The House Ferret

Ferrets adapt well to living indoors. However, they will require a cage where they can be safely locked in when they are left alone in the house. A litter tray (or trays) must be provided, preferably one with a low entrance and a high back as ferrets usually reverse into a corner to defecate (See page 27, Litter training).

Ferret-proofing Your Home

Ferrets are extremely inquisitive and can wriggle into seemingly impossible gaps and spaces. Before allowing your ferret to roam:
• Block up all holes and check where pipes emerge.
• Radiators should be fitted with a cover to prevent the ferret getting trapped behind.
• Gas fires will need a removable, ventilated guard.
• Drawers and cupboard doors will need child-proof locks.
• Beware of furniture that ferrets can climb into or under – there are heartbreaking stories of ferrets being accidentally crushed.

Give your ferret a chance to explore his new surroundings.

• Make sure appliances such as washing machines and dish-washers are not accessible to your ferret.

Remember, a ferret can squeeze through tiny gaps and spaces.

A good tip is to lie on the floor and imagine you are able to squeeze into any gaps greater than an inch or two! You will soon see what has to be done!

Settling In

When you first arrive home, place your ferret in his cage with a dish of food and fresh water, and allow him to explore his new surroundings. When he has settled, you can allow him to investigate the rest of the house.

The correct way to hold a ferret.

Handling

A ferret should not be approached in a tentative and hesitant way. If you draw your hand back suddenly he may nip, thinking that your hand is food. Ferrets have very poor sight and mistakes can be made.

The correct way to pick up a ferret is to grasp him across the shoulder with the index finger pointing up the neck towards the head, and the thumb and rest of the fingers under the ferret's forelegs. The ferret should be handled gently but firmly.

17

The House Ferret

With time and patience, you can build up a real rapport.

A large hob or pregnant jill should be supported with a hand under their rear quarters. It is almost impossible for a ferret to bite when held in this way.

A ferret will soon learn that being handled is fun and will enjoy being cuddled and tickled behind the ears. Stroke him and talk quietly to him. Just like kittens and puppies, ferrets tend to 'test' things with their teeth. They are not being vicious; it is a means of experimenting. So, until you have got to know your ferret, don't allow him too close to your face.

When you and your ferret have built up a real rapport, you should be able to pick him up by placing your hand under his chest, and, eventually, your ferret may even like being carried around draped across your shoulders.

Gaining Confidence

If your ferret tries to nip your fingers, don't alarm him by making quick movements or shouting. Take things slowly, and allow your ferret time to get to know you. A ferret from a rescue shelter may have previously suffered rough treatment from uncaring owners, and it may take a while to gain his confidence.

Offer food treats, and stroke him gently while he eats. You have to show your ferret that he need not be afraid of you. Time and patience is needed, but eventually you will be rewarded with a trusting, affectionate pet. There are very few 'nasty' ferrets, only scared ferrets who have been badly treated.

Youngsters

Very young ferrets are tearaways – they think that everything was made for trying their teeth out! This is not viciousness, only rough play. Puppies and kittens have to learn that biting is not acceptable, and young ferrets (kits) have to be persuaded that chomping fingers is not the done thing. Play-biting is different from fear-biting, and a light tap on the nose and a firm "No" is usually all that is required to teach good manners.

Routine

Ferrets are creatures of habit. They appreciate a routine of regular feeding, cleaning and play-times, so try to establish a programme of care for your ferret. This will help him become accustomed to his new home.

Introducing The Family

Meeting Other Ferrets

Although ferrets are gregarious, they do not always mix well with strangers and may become aggressive. Therefore it is not advisable to allow your pet to meet other ferrets unless they are going to live together.

If you do want to introduce a new ferret, stick to these simple rules:

• Keep the newcomer separately for the first 10 days to avoid any risk of illness transmission. This will also help your new ferret to settle in and get used to you.

• Then, under careful supervision, place the two ferrets together in a room or area neither know well. Provide a dish containing a special treat for them to share.

• It is also common for one (usually the 'old timer') to try to drag the newcomer by the neck. Providing this is not too rough, it can be regarded as establishing a pecking order. It will frequently turn into play. However, if it seems too rough and causes squeals of fear, or the 'skunking' of scent spray out of fear or alarm, intervene and separate the two. Try again later - they will gradually become accustomed to each other.

• As a rule, younger ferrets accept newcomers more readily than older ones so think carefully if you wish to introduce a youngster. Entire males should never be expected to live together.

DID YOU KNOW?

Ferrets owned by a psychologist at the University of Warwick, England, have been used as therapy animals to help autistic children, and to calm the nerves of children awaiting surgery.

The Family And Other Animals!

Most ferrets will be happy to meet all the family as soon as they have settled in, but remember that just as there are shy people, there are shy ferrets. Children should always be supervised when handling ferrets.

Your ferret will also need to meet your other pets. Cats are usually fascinated but prefer to watch from a distance, and they can take off to the top of a chair if the ferret pesters them.

Dogs need careful supervision – one snap could seriously injure or kill a ferret, while a frightened ferret can inflict a painful bite to a dog's nose. Keep your dog on a lead for the initial meeting. Most dogs and ferrets eventually learn mutual respect, and some even play or sleep together.

DID YOU KNOW?

The Ermine Portrait by Nicholas Hilliard of Queen Elizabeth I probably features a pet ferret rather than a stoat.

Feeding Your Ferret

The ferret is a carnivore, which means its main diet should be meat. It has a very short gut, roughly three hours from input to output, and requires a high protein diet to enable it to get as much nutrition from its food as possible.

Types Of Food

There are many dry, complete ferret foods available, but you may prefer more natural feeding, in which case the meat should be given raw.

• Rabbit: fed whole, it contains everything that a ferret needs – protein, vitamins and minerals.
• Poultry: chicken provides fat, minerals and protein.
• Liver: can be fed in small quantities once a week.
• Lamb's heart and kidneys: can be given twice a week.
• Mince (chopped beef): a useful standby, but it does not contain all the protein and vitamins needed.
• Fish: do not give your ferret salty, very oily or cured fish. Fish such as cod, whiting and flat fish can be fed safely, but be sure to remove the gut and fillet the fish.
• Eggs: as a treat, once a week. Too many eggs can cause baldness.
• Milk: not recommended. It makes for smelly and very loose droppings. Watering the milk down can reduce the laxative effect.

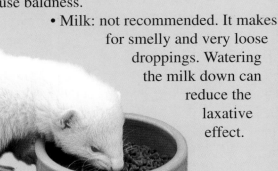

A complete dry food is available for ferrets.

Many ferret keepers feed a combination of dry and fresh food. Dry food is more hygienic in hot weather when flies are attracted to meat. Clean water must be available at all times, especially if feeding a dry diet.

Eggs can be fed as an occasional treat.

Quantities

There are no hard and fast rules on how much to feed your ferret as there are so many factors to be taken into account. Ferrets can range in size from 1lb to 5.5 lbs, so if you use a dry feed follow the manufacturer's guidelines.

Only give meat to your pet when he is in his cage. Ferrets tend to stash things away for later, and it is easier to find the hidden food if you restrict his movements.

Kits can eat two or three times more than adults, and all ferrets tend to eat less in hot weather.

Treats

Some ferrets enjoy a piece of fruit, such as apple or banana. All enjoy vanilla ice cream, but it should only be allowed in very small quantities.

Ferrets love ice cream – but it should be restricted to small quantities.

Caring For Your Ferret

Cleaning The Cage

Do this daily. Ferrets are very clean animals and will only use one corner of their cage for a latrine. But bedding should be checked to ensure that your ferret is not stashing uneaten food, especially if raw meat is included in their diet. Once a week, the cage should be scrubbed with a 'ferret safe' mild disinfectant. Sterilising fluid for baby equipment is ideal.

Grooming

Ferrets do not usually need grooming. Some tolerate being brushed but ferrets are usually too busy to sit still!

However, grooming provides a good opportunity to check for parasites such as fleas and ticks. If you see little black specks of 'flea dirt' in the fur, you should obtain a spray from your vet. A tick will usually drop off if soaked in surgical spirit. Make sure that no part of the tick remains embedded in the skin.

Bathing

Most ferrets do not enjoy being bathed; it is not usually necessary and can make your ferret smelly! Too much bathing depletes the coat's natural oils and the ferret's glands then work overtime to replace them.

Some ferrets enjoy playing in water - but bathing is rarely popular, and it is mostly unnecessary.

If you do need to bath your ferret use a shampoo for kittens or rabbits (or human babies!), but never a dog shampoo. You might also consider a dry ferret shampoo such as 'Ferretsheen' as this is less stressful for the animal.

Before clipping.

Nails

Most ferrets like digging when given the opportunity and this helps to keep the nails short. However, they may need trimming every two or three weeks, although the nails on the back feet will only require clipping as the ferret gets older. You can use ordinary nail-clippers to keep the nails trim. Most ferrets have pale nails and it is easy to see the pink 'quick' or blood vessel. Clip just below this blood vessel, taking care not to pinch or cut it. Ask someone to hold the ferret securely while you clip.

Use guillotine style nail-clippers to keep the nails in trim.

Teeth

A ferret that is fed a correct diet and not given sugary treats should not suffer from undue build up of tartar on their teeth. However, older ferrets do need careful checks to their teeth and gums. Swollen gums or badly discoloured teeth signal the need to consult your vet.

After clipping.

Training Your Ferret

Harness And Lead Training

Most ferrets love to walk on a harness and lead, but they need to become accustomed to this and may be reluctant to begin with. When first harnessing your ferret, try to distract him with a treat. Once the harness is fitted, allow him to inspect it, and try another treat to take his mind off the feel of it.

Next clip the lead onto the harness and carry your ferret to somewhere stimulating, such as the garden. Let him wander freely while you follow on the end of the lead. In fact, most ferrets always expect you to follow them, so don't expect a straightforward walk of your choosing!

Step One.

Step Three.

Step Two.

Step Four.

DID YOU KNOW?

Ferrets can sleep so soundly that even experienced keepers are alarmed when they pick up the sleeping, limp ferret. The condition is commonly referred to as "sleeping not dead syndrome". It can sometimes take several minutes to wake the ferret, who will just yawn and look a bit surprised at all the fuss.

Ferrets love burrowing through fallen leaves, undergrowth and long grass so be prepared to allow them their own pace whilst they explore. If your ferret simply lies down and refuses to move, be patient and do not drag him along. Ferrets are rarely still for long.

If you walk your ferret in a park, be alert for dogs and be prepared to pick up your ferret to keep him out of harm's way.

Never allow your ferret to roam without a lead. Ferrets have no homing instinct and will soon become lost.

Litter Training

Ferrets are easily house-trained as they naturally select one or two corners to use as their toilet. However, they will tell you which corner - and there is little room for negotiation. You can line the corner with paper, a plastic mat or put a litter tray in it.

Ferrets are intelligent animals, and respond well to certain types of training.

Health Care

Abscesses

Ferrets are susceptible to abscesses caused by bites, stings, scratches or injuries that become infected. Treatment, which should be undertaken by your vet, involves lancing the abscess and thorough draining, followed by a course of antibiotics.

Cancers/Tumours

Ferrets are prone to all types of tumours – benign and malignant. If you notice or feel any lumps on your ferret take him to the vet. It may be just superficial and treatable with surgery.

Canine Distemper

Canine distemper is a major killer of ferrets. Unless they are protected by vaccination, they run a very real risk of contracting the disease when out walking or by being handled by someone who has been in contact with an unvaccinated dog. Typical signs are: running eyes, gummed-up lids, mucoid nasal discharge and lack of appetite. Immediate veterinary attention may prevent death but the disease is usually fatal.

Colds And 'Flu

If you have a cold or 'flu you should avoid your ferret as he can catch it from you. Symptoms in ferrets are pretty much the same as those in humans; fever, lack of appetite and sneezing.

Diarrhoea

This might simply be caused by what your ferret has eaten or it may be a sign of an underlying disease. Milk, eggs and ice cream can produce loose droppings, and if you suspect that this is the cause you can take first-aid steps. Starve your ferret for 24 hours, making sure that he has access to plenty of fresh water. However, if there are any signs of blood or mucus in the stools, take a sample and your ferret to the vet.

Ear Mites

If you notice the build up of smelly dark-coloured wax or brown granular specks in the outer ear of your pet, it is more than likely a sign of ear mites. Your ferret may scratch his ears and, in extreme cases, he may hold his head tilted to one side, lose his balance and turn in circles. If left untreated, collapse and death is the final outcome. Caught in the early stages, treatment is straightforward by the use of ear-drops or an injection prescribed by your veterinary surgeon.

Health Care

Heatstroke

Like dogs, ferrets cannot sweat, and generally have an inefficient body cooling system. Keep the cage out of direct sunshine, and in hot weather provide shallow bowls of water for them to cool off in. Heat exhaustion can occur in temperatures in excess of 80F. A ferret with heatstroke appears distressed, stretching out and seeming to have difficulty breathing. Complete collapse, coma and death will follow if prompt action is not taken.

Remove the ferret from the hot environment into a shady cool place. Roll him in cool (not very cold) water to revive him and contact your vet.

Intestinal Blockages

Symptoms include vomiting, anorexia, complete inability to pass faeces or being able to pass only thin, thread-like stools. Urgent veterinary treatment is required.

Jills ills

Jills are susceptible to a variety of illnesses. Being left in oestrus (season) can result in a jill developing bone marrow disease (aplastic anaemia). Symptoms include lethargy and anorexia, and the outcome is

usually fatal. The best way to avoid this disease is to have your jill spayed.

Pyometra is a condition in which the lining of the womb produces large quantities of purulent secretions. Symptoms are a high temperature, poor appetite and excessive thirst. The only treatment is a complete spay.

Vitamin Problems

With the introduction of complete ferret foods, it should not be necessary to include extra vitamins in your ferret's diet – unless the ferret is pregnant, convalescing, or if advised by your vet. Some vitamins are stored in the body and 'overdosing' could lead to problems. Be very cautious when adding supplements and do not overdo the treats.

IF IN DOUBT...

Consult a vet as soon as you can. Ferrets can decline in health very rapidly and tomorrow may be too late.

DID YOU KNOW?

Ferret kits of three weeks old will start eating raw meat, such as day-old chicks, before their eyes are even open.

DID YOU KNOW?

It is a complete fallacy that a ferret must be vicious and half-starved to be able to be used for hunting.